CW01238157

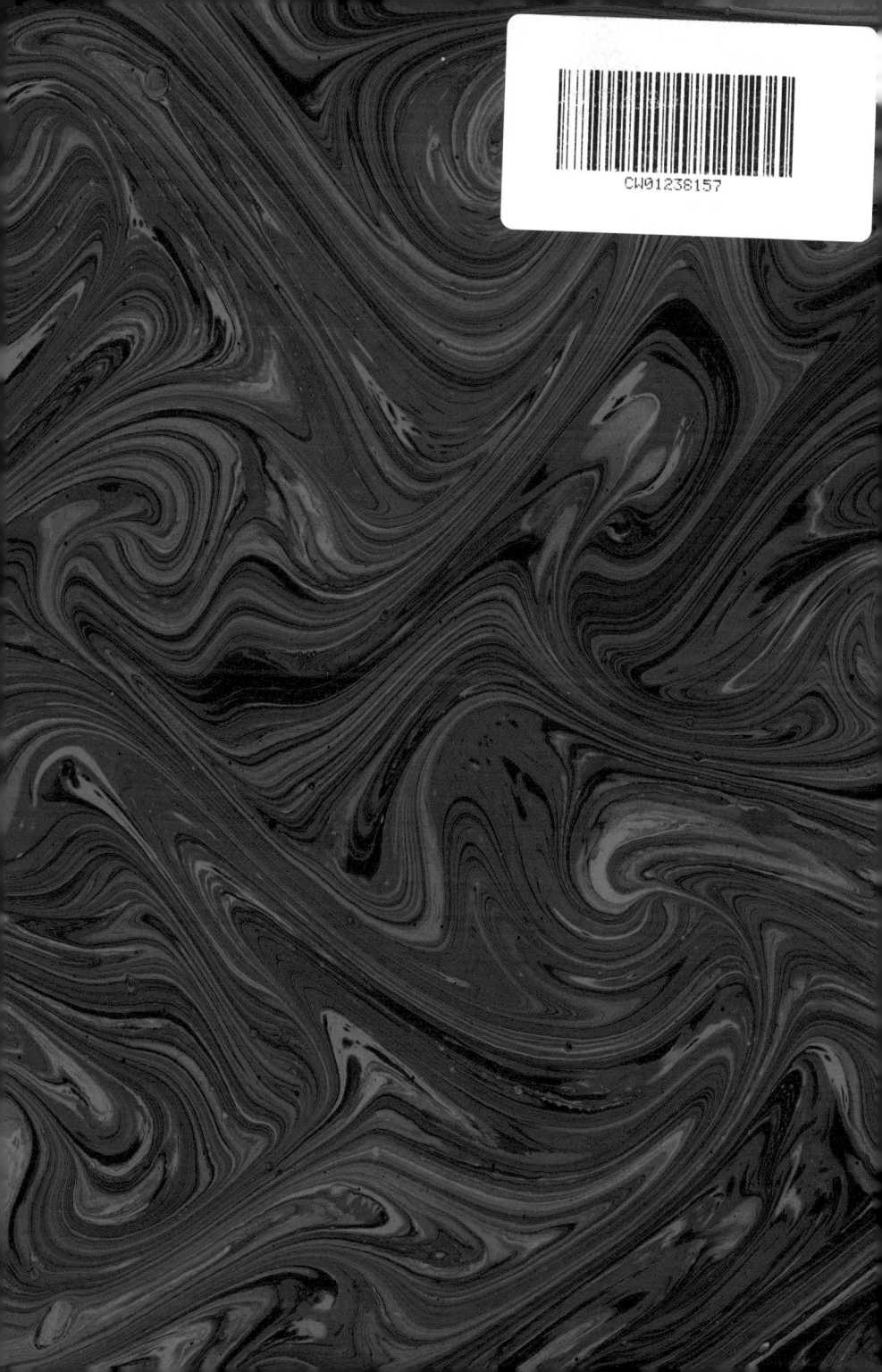

Monkey - Puzzle

for Wendy

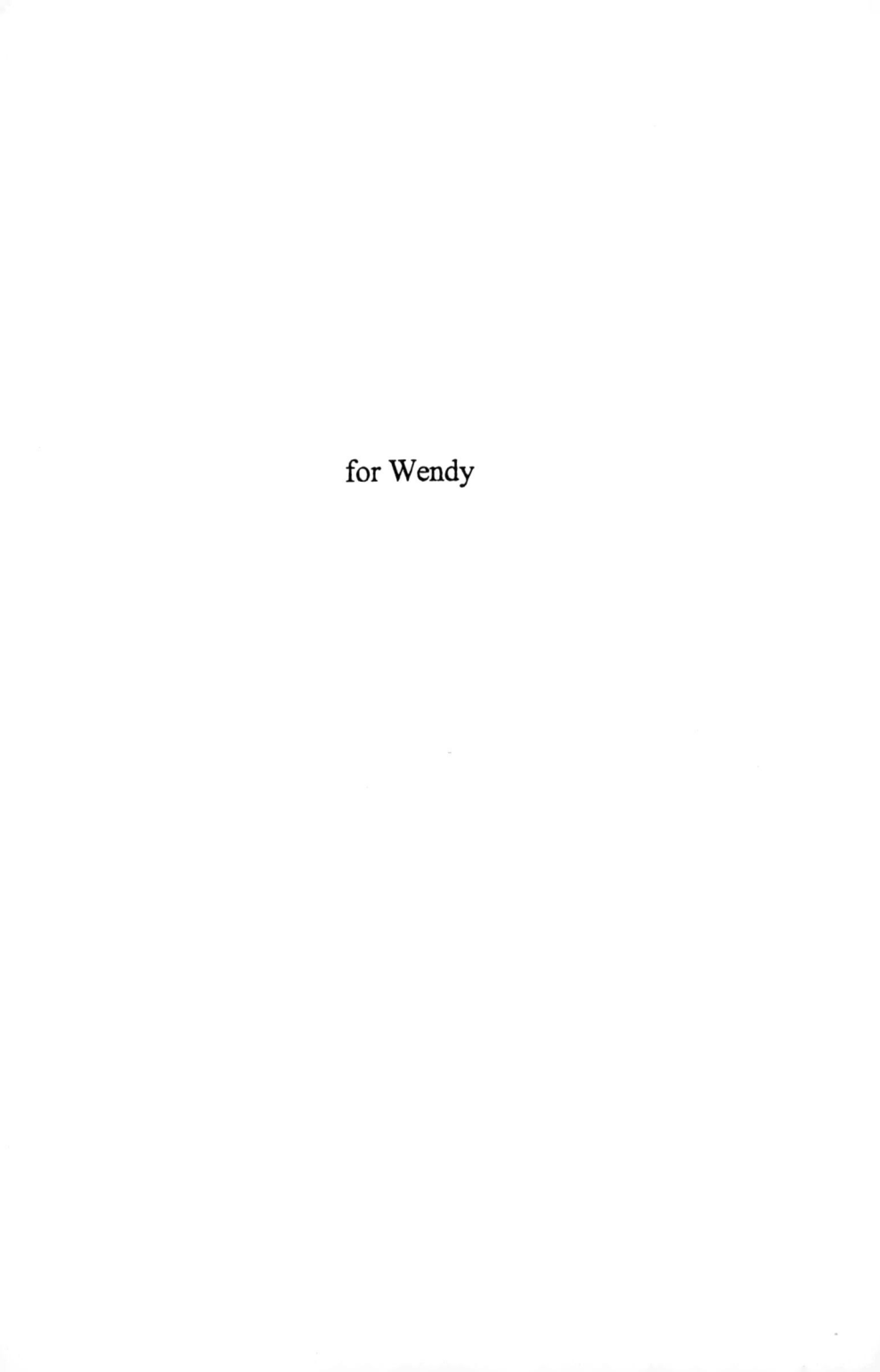

The Monkey-Puzzle,

.. an experiment in allegory.

TONY COX

Ismailia : 1 September, 1952.

Jebeldali

ISBN: 0 9511018 1 1

All rights reserved. No part of this publication may be reproduced in any form or by any means without the prior permission of the publishers

Published by: Jebeldali Press
                No.3, Bastwell House,
                BLACKBURN
                Lancashire. BB1 9TE

Copyright © Tony Cox 2002

Printed in England by: Thomas Briggs (Blackburn) Ltd
                         37 King Street,
                         Blackburn
                         Lancs BB2 2DH

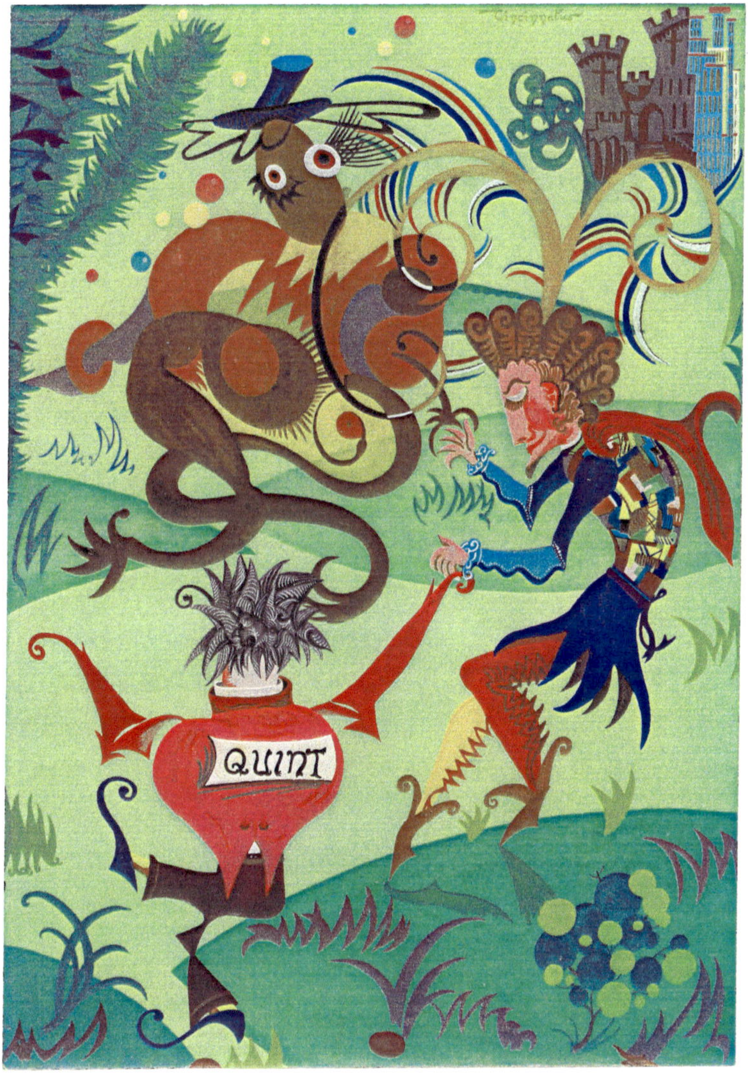
QUINT

Contents

Preface	9
Introduction	12
I	17
II	55

Preface . .

I wove ten thousand million dancing dreams
    and three came true;
but one — the dearest, fairest of the three —
    eclipsed the other two.
Transcending every highest high it dazzled me,
    eluding all description.

And so it is that when I try
to outline my first tentative philosophy,
I am defeated from the start
and at the best can only make a heartless
    ever-folded triptych.

The diamond centrepiece, concealed
yet by its very nearness throwing into sharp relief
the outer doors, may never be revealed
but must remain the symbol of a true belief
— the indescribable sustaining force
— a faith — a sacred opalescent horse
unseen behind the temple's altar-wraps,
invisible in closest guarded sanctity.

    the hidden symbol of my true belief,
    my God, perhaps . . . perhaps . . . .

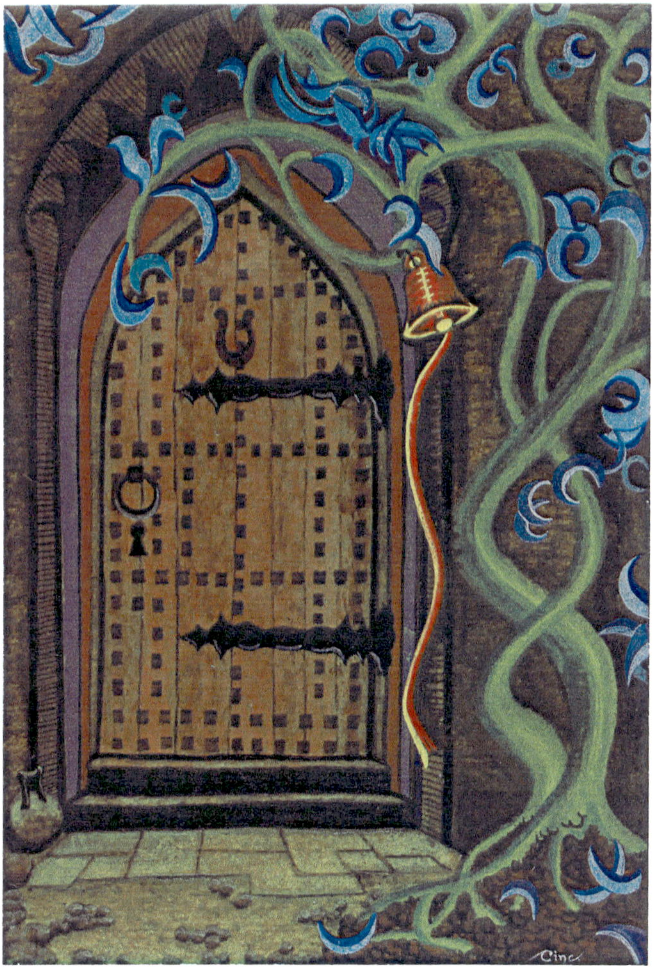
Cinc

Introduction . .

Look up, look out,
look over the head of the layabout,
stretch into the sky and sing and shout.

O leave your friends to dig in the sand,
set out for the rose-tipped mountain top;
set off today to where, they say,
one may glimpse the Promised Land.

Some are led to the Door by the People-who-Know,
while others stumble across it by chance,
but me and my shadow were lost in a storm
when we found the Door, the Inscrutable Door
to Romance.

Wander far and long through Valley
towards the tantalising rose-tipped mountain peaks
ahead, and there, where the hurly stream
of pilgrims seems lost in a whirlpool,
perhaps you will find it.

It's there, somewhere, and still and forever
the hopeful upward drift will divide at the whirlpool
for some to go on to the rose-tipped mountains
while others go round by the Door.

I found the Door, the Inscrutable Door
when lost in a storm.
It opened easily though I did not ring the bell
and I entered the gloomy, narrow passage
glad of the shelter it afforded.

There was a tiny star at the farther end
which grew very bright as I hurried towards it
and proved to be sunlight
reflected from distant mountain ice.
I ran too fast, and as I emerged
from the passage out into the sun and snow,
I tripped and fell . . and fell . . and fell
to the valley floor far below.

I awoke with a bump on my head
and a song in my heart,
for the sun was strong on the back of my neck
and the timothy grass blew apart
to reveal a splendid view
of the rose-tipped mountains
— but now from the other side.

What glory a mountain can hide.

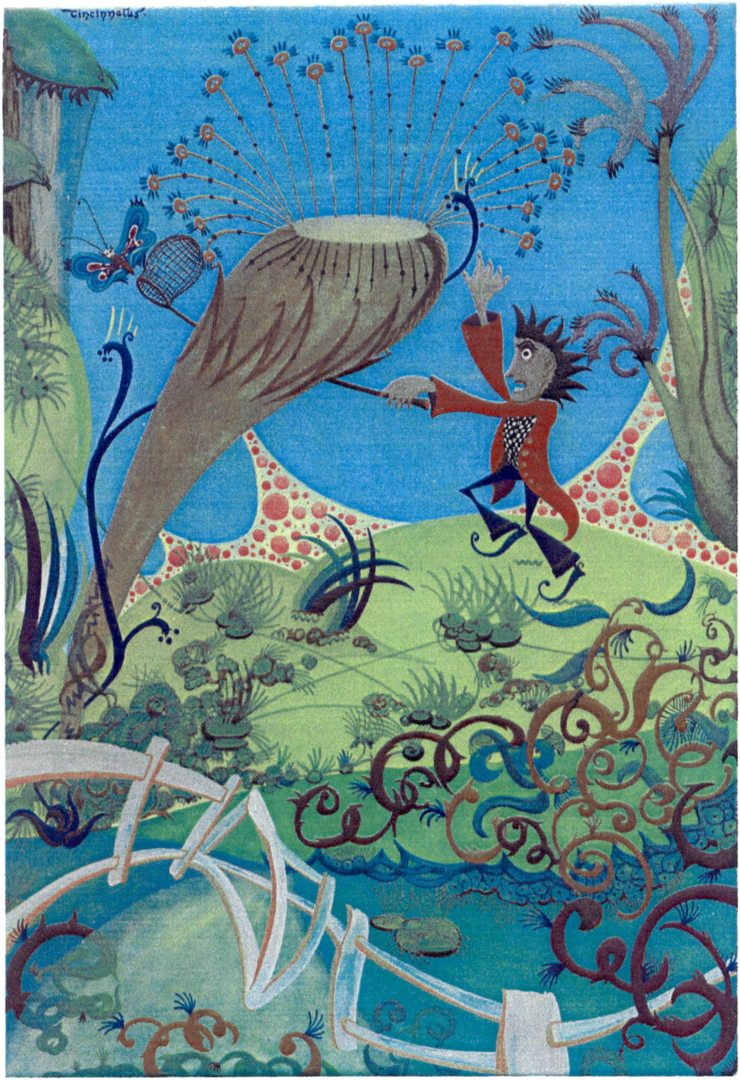
Cincinnatus

I

    Suddenly a little man two feet tall,
wearing gay trousers and a black-and-white check
waistcoat, shot into sight from behind the small,
green-wooded hillock on my left. He burbled happily
to himself as he chased after a brilliant golden
butterfly which fluttered lazily just beyond the reach
of his eagerly outstretched net.

Although his little legs did their utmost to keep up
with him, the task was too much for them
and he fell over: tumbleturvey he rolled down the
slope into a clump of gorse. Picking himself
out carefully, he brushed the dead leaves from
his coat, retrieved his butterfly net from the lower
branches of a nearby tree and, twittering meekly
the while, he took from his pocket an extensive
white handkerchief: mopped his brow.

Meanwhile, another golden butterfly had appeared,
intoxicated what with all the honey and the dew
and the gleeful sunshine and everything. Full of
joy, it settled on a huge buttercup and began
preening its antennae in a most provocative manner.

The little man spied it
and stopped his twittering at once.
Seizing his net, he made a valiant rush at it
— or rather he *would* have done had not
his foot been caught in a fold of his preposterous
handkerchief.
Again he tumbled to the ground.

I watched for a little while as the heap of handkerchief,
butterfly net and muffled expostulations squirmed and
rolled about, succeeding only in becoming more and
more hopelessly involved.
Then I extricated him. He was very red in the face and
out-of-breath, and he had to sit down for
many minutes with his tongue lolling out, gulping
great gulps of air, before he was sufficiently
recovered. Then he darted off quickly, emitting a
peculiarly penetrating whistle. Almost at once he
returned with another little man.

"Chorus!" he yelled, seeing me, and he rushed at
me, tripping and falling headlong as he did so.
(What he would have done to me had he not
fallen I cannot imagine.)

While he picked himself up and the other consoled him,
nine more similar little men came puffing round the
corner of the hill, each complete with brightly
coloured jacket and trousers, black-and-white check
waistcoat, butterflynet and, as I now noticed for
the first time, each with a white card sewn to
the back of his coat bearing a name.

The first little man was Double Faggot,
the second one Dulcianus.
The others were Piccolo, Night Horn,
Full Bone, High Wood, Knee Echo,
Clear-Handsome, Little Willow, Beautiful Burden
and Lovely Closed.

Curious names . . . .

They sat themselves down crosslegged on the ground.
So small they were that I could hardly see them
there in the long timothy grass, though I could
hear them quite plainly:
"He's Chorus," insisted Dulcianus.
"Fiddlesticks," said Lovely Closed, "he's just Ordinary
Folk."
"Well, maybe," Dulcianus consented, "but he's not
good Ordinary Folk, nor even *ordinary* Ordinary Folk,
that he is'n't, or he'd chase butterflies."
"Fiddlesticks," said Lovely Closed again, "he's just fed up
with butterflies, that's what . . . like me," he added
suddenly. "Silly old butterflies . . . ridiclus silly
potty old butterflies . . . Why! I've only caught one
in a week; and that bit me!"

He showed the glowering Dulcianus a red mark on his hand.
"Why! your butterfly idea is just plain silly-potty, so
there . . . fiddlesticks!" and Lovely Closed stood up, defiant,
as though daring anyone to dispute his words.
Far from disputing his words, the other nine little
men stood up also:
"Fiddlesticks!" they shouted, "Silly! Potty! Nasty vicious
ol' butterflies!" and they completely drowned out the
protestations of Dulcianus who was adamant nevertheless.

Lovely Closed turned to me, and the remaining ten
were silent as he spoke:
"Excuse me, but are you Ordinary Folk or Chorus?"
"I think I'm quite an ordinary folk," I answered,
and went on to explain the circumstances of my
arrival in their land.
"Liar, liar," screamed Dulcianus, and he made
another rush at me, only to be seized and
held back by three of the little men. He cooled
down at once and they let him go.

The others, after staring at me for a time,
apparently decided that I was harmless and they
all began speaking together:

"I would rather like to show you my poem," said
Double Faggot timidly.

"I have a theory which will interest you," said Knee Echo.

"Come, come into the treetops with me, and
gain everlasting happiness and health," said High Wood.

"Silence, everyone," roared Lovely Closed; and
everyone was quiet except Dulcianus who at
that moment fell down a hidden pit, letting
out a shriek of surprise and anger. There
was a thud as he reached the bottom and
Lovely Closed strode over to the place:

"Shut up! Shut up, down there!" he cried,
(though not a sound he heard confused the air
besides the sulky twitter-bird).

"Tick . . . tock . . . tick . . . " said Beautiful
Burden, breathing with excitement.

Lovely Closed returned:
"I shall introduce you one by one."

There was a murmur of approval and consent.

"I am Lovely Closed; faithful subject of His Majesty King One-and-a-half, whom you will meet later perhaps."

"How d'ye do?"

"How d'ye do.
This is Double Faggot; he writes poetry."

Double Faggot stepped forward and bowed. There was a cat on his shoulder which I had not noticed before. It lost its balance and nearly fell off as he bowed. It overbalanced completely and fell to the ground when he stood up straight again.
"How d'ye do."

"This is Waves of the Sea, my cat," he said, picking it up and replacing it on his shoulder. It nodded at me condescendingly but did not speak. "My cat is an affable cat, as the first man said . . . eh? Would you care to hear my poem?"

I was about to reply
that I'd be delighted
to hear his poem
when Lovely Closed interrupted:

" . . and this is Knee Echo,
the inventor," he said,
introducing a man with dark
watery eyes and spectacles
set on the tip of his nose.
"How d'ye do."

"How d'ye do."

"I would be very much obliged
if you were to tap my head,
 . here .. " he said,
and pointing to the shiny bald part
right on top
he proffered me a tiny hammer.

All the other little men
gathered about us to watch,
so I took the hammer
and tapped gently with it
on the smooth surface
he had indicated.

"Harder," he said.

The hammer grew bigger
and I tapped a little harder.

"Harder!" he snapped.

I did as I was told
and the hammer continued growing.

"Harder, harder!!" he shouted,
and giant tears rolled down his cheeks
as I struck him again
and again
with ever-increasing force.

"Harder!!!" he screamed.

The hammer was so big
and heavy now
that I could only just
manage to swing it round
then
Suddenly
his head cracked open . . .

It was quite empty
except for another, smaller
head.

"How d'ye do!" said the smaller head.

"How d'ye do," I said.

"How curious . . . ," I thought
and the thinking of it must have held me
preoccupied a minute for I remembered little of
what the other men did:

Piccolo, proclaimed as the King's left hand
man, was worried about something and he
ran in small circles muttering strangely.
Night Horn did'n't speak but just rolled his
enormous deep eyes as he looked at me.
Dulcianus would not be introduced, but
scowled ferociously, limping in the background
slashing at the bushes with his tattered
butterflynet. "You pushed me down that hole,"
he might have said; or it could have
been "How d'ye do" in a tone which
implied the former.

Clear-Handsome, Little Willow and Full Bone
wanted me to call them Andy, Willy and
Boney and would I care to make up
a foursome at tennis? I regretted that I
did not play tennis very well.
High Wood climbed a tree
to hang upside down by his heels like a bat.
"That does me good,"
said High Wood.

"And this is Beautiful Burden," said Lovely
Closed, bringing forward the last little man.
"He's gaumless," he added, and sighed wearily.
(Not a very nice thing to say, but
Beautiful Burden did'n't seem to mind.)
"How d'ye do," I said.
"Tick . . . tock . . " said Beautiful Burden.

Tick . , tock . . .

Tick, tock, the human clock (Homunculus),
the little man among the little men;
say that again.

"Tick . , tock . . . . "

For the rest of the morning and half the afternoon
we played and talked, those ten little men and I.
Then, as we were resting after the fifth
strenuous game of leapfrog, a voice came
striding through the woods behind us.
The little men ran to hide.
The owner of the voice appeared — another
little man, this time with grey hair:
"Alright Boney, I can see you," he shouted,
"and you, Beautiful Burden. I'm not blind.
Come on out, the rest of you."

They crept modestly into being.

"This must be King One-and-a-half," I thought.

I thought wrong.

Seeing me, he said "I'm Quint, right hand man
to King One-and-a-half.
How d'ye do."
Turning to the others before I could answer,
he went on:

"His Majesty, His Royal Highness King One-and-a-half
 will suffer Himself to hear your
songs now; and, all being satisfactory, He
will afterwards favour you with the première
performance of His own very latest exclusive
royal masterpiece.
Come along.
He's waiting, so we'd better hurry."

They led me over the hillock, up a steep
lane, over a gate and across a field of
Meadowsweet, of Butterbur, of Lady's Mantle,
to a very bright green lawn with a row of
bushes and tree stumps down each side
and with a slight rise at the far end.

Surmounting this rise sat yet another little
man with a black-and-white check
waistcoat. He wore a most hideous palegreen-
and-purple-striped jacket and cherry trousers.
He was different from the others in that
he had long whiskers and a silly little
crown perched atop his head. AND he was,
I estimated, about *three* feet tall whereas
the others were *two* feet only.

King One-and-a-half, obviously.

The little men all bowed low as they neared
him and then sat crosslegged on the lawn.
I did likewise and the meeting began.

Each little man in turn stood up and sang
a number of songs of his own composition.
Each one, that is, except Double Faggot the
poet, who refused to set his poem to
music. He said that would spoil it and
I suspect he knew best.

They sang the usual songs
which little men so often sing:
of ogres, flittermice and fields in Spring,
and love and eagles on the wing;
of prison towers, magic bells,
and poisoned wine and wishing wells,
black witches spelling evil spells;
of midnight revels, gorgeous feasts,
and angels, devils, beauties, beasts;
of country gardens, lilting fountains,
rainbows, tigers, fearless mountains,
gypsy violins and ships at sea,
and blood, and tears, and brides-to-be.

All these they sang with dozens more
— they made poor Double Faggot snore,
yet still they sing, they sing, they sing
their songs to One-and-a-half, their King
— who never heard one word.

At last the final song was well and truly sung
and Quint stood up to proclaim
the climax — His Majesty King One-and-a-half
had very graciously agreed to sing
His own latest personal masterpiece.

Amid thunderous applause
King One-and-a-half arose, adjusted His crown
and looked about His audience.

He frowned a regal frown
whereupon
Ceased the clapping and shouting . .

He felt in the right hand pocket of His
black-and-white check waistcoat and fished
out His spectacles.
He put them on.

I.   Cincinnatus.

He cleared His royal throat,
and fanning a speck of dust
from His royal coat
began:

    "Polliwig, polliwog,
        gobbling, wriggling,
What are you at when you grow
        to a giggling
             frilliwig?

    Boggling frollywog,
        gillitwig tumbling,
Why do that when you know
        that the fumbling
           silly big

frog that you see on the bogside,
        fat and slow,
    grumpy and goggle-eyed,
was a jolly polliwig – just like you –
        not long ago?

    How d'ye do."

"How d'ye do," cried Quint and Piccolo;
all the others answered too,
so: "How d'ye do," or "How d'ye do,"
or "How d'ye do, Sir, how d'ye do."

Frenzied applause again and calls of "Encore,
encore!"

Pink with success and looking very foolish and
ridiculous, King One-and-a-half raised his hand
for silence. The tumult subsided and he
sang another song:

> "Who will agree
>   and say with me
>   that trees are sly?
>   Who'll deny it,
>   and why?
>
> Appletrees, pears
>   and lightweight chairs
>   have torn the sky,
>   pierced the Earth
>   and drunk her dry.

>	Holly and oak
>	and peeping folk
>		are old and shy,
>			yet they can do it
>				who try . .
>
> Hey howa! we'll sing, and never say die
>	(ring hollow my laughter),
> for I am the King and nought better than I
>	will follow hereafter.
>
>	Hickory dee
>	the hornbeam tree
>		has grown so high
>		that Jacks-in-Green
>		must learn to fly.
>		When they have done it
>		so can we
>	Hey howa! howa! howa!!"

I was turning away, disappointed, when something caught mine eye. Looking more closely, I noticed that the King's whiskers were false. Could I not see clearly the string which held them on?

Now the little men had said:
"We made Him King because He has long whiskers.
Whiskers are wise and much to be respected.
King One-and-a-half has whiskers as long-and-a-half
as any of us. So One-and-a-half is King."

And here I saw that the whiskers were not
true – no more true than his smirking face,
so I rushed upon him to fling off his deception,
the mask, and I tugged and tugged at his
wretchèd hair
but there it stayed.

The string I'd thought to hold his whiskers on
was there still, and now I saw that
the string was to hold his crown in place . .
He had real whiskers . . . a real face.

This unprovoked assault upon their King
left the twelve little men and the Chorus too
with nothing of doubt as to what to do.
They set about me with their sticks
and beat me with their little arms,
they kicked me with their puny legs

until, too weak and ill
with loss of blood from my wounded pride,
I sank exhausted to the ground . .
I died in agony.

      *   *   *   *   *   *   *

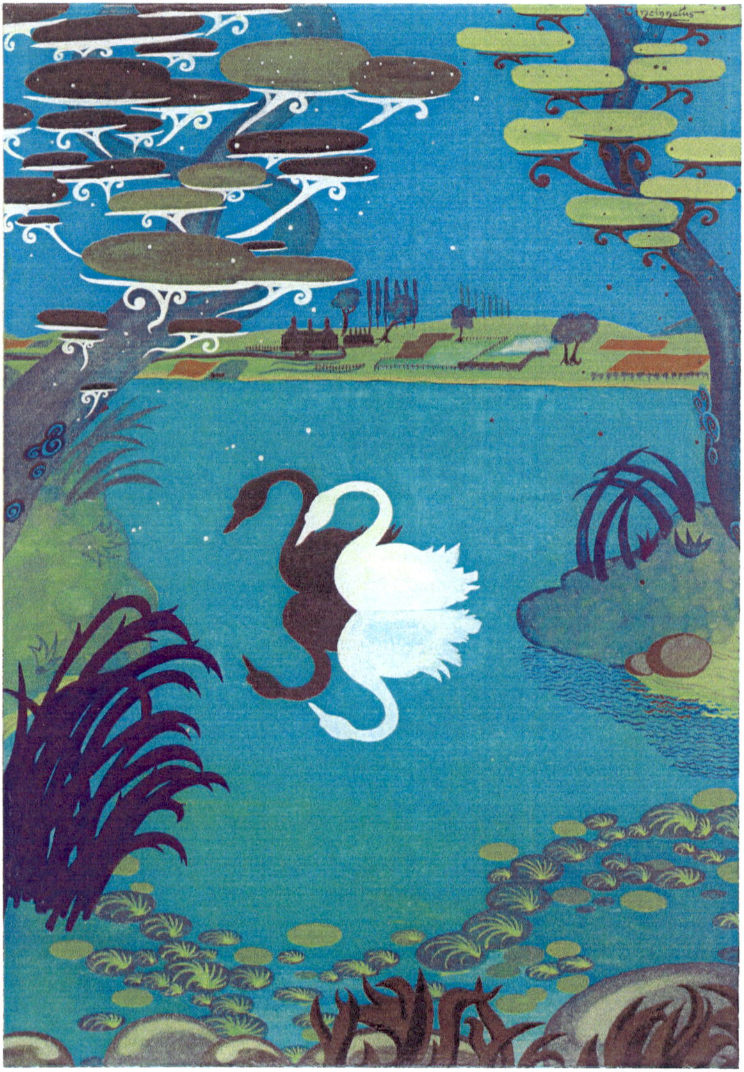

I picked myself up once more.
King One-and-a-half and his twelve little men
were gone,
but the sun still shone
as bright as before.
(And that's what matters in dreams of mine
— the sun must shine.)

I walked along a winding lane beside a stream
and saw four swans, two black, two white;
the white ones white as the full moon's beam,
the black ones blacker than Night himself.
I came across an open sunlit dell
and sat on a stone to think,
I watched as a delicate shy gazelle
passed by to cool itself — to drink
at the nearby pool.

It bowed its graceful head: it drank.
Refreshed and cheered
it settled on the grassy bank
and gently disappeared.

I looked again,

and there, reclining in its place
was Double Faggot with his cat,
a sweet, seraphic smile upon his face —
in such a mellow, gliding, glowing humour that
he called me to his side
to tell me of his poem:

"My poem is deep and wide and long.
Its hands are sympathetic, yet as strong
as doctors' hands when taking mine and leading me
to see the shining land of Reverie
where I belong.

It shows me the whispering whin on the edge of time
and the murmur of age;
it shows me the sycamore tree on the rim of glad space
and a glittering cage;
it shows me the slow, miraculous expanse of slime
and the tarnished page,
and it shows me the sphinx's ever-watching face.

Such things as these I'd never seen before
except in the staring eyes of a blind old man.
He told me of a lonely distant shore
but his voice was strange and I'd fled from him; I ran
to my sister who lives by the stream
— my sister to whom I never lied.
She never spoke nor even thought of space nor time,
but she understood me when I cried.

I was younger then and I could not see
that the old man's finger pointed at me
on the lonely distant shore.
I'd never heard such a thing before.

My poem is wide and long and deep.
Its whiskers sensitively probe and search the creeping
inner, darker depths of things:
instinctively it brings the jewels there to light
— to share, to keep.

It brings me the stars hidden deep in the grooves of night
in disconsolate cloud;
it brings me the turbulent waves of an underground sea
which the silence has plowed;
it brings me sparkling fire from the hooves of a fight
with its shadowy crowd,
and it brings me the truth and the truth of me.

Such things as these had always seemed before
so unimportant: fleas on the fleas in the coat of a dog.
I thought the men who hunted at the core
were mad to hope for gold in a rotten log;
but still, of course, they do - and find it there.

I was younger then and I did not mind;
I did not care for the hidden things, and more
— I'd never been to that lonely distant shore.

My poem is long and deep and wide,
with room for everyone and everything inside.

It has big eyes like mine to see
intensively — to be intensified."

Having finished, Double Faggot fixed his
attention on a remote object and began to
pluck idly at the fur behind the cat's ears.

"He is evidently awaiting my criticism,"
I thought. "Poets are very easily upset . . . perhaps
if I just show an interest in the poem
without attempting a criticism . . . . "
On second and third considerations this seemed the
wisest course to adopt (for I could hardly
criticize a poem which I had not properly
understood. In fact I was'n't really sure whether
he had actually recited his poem or whether he had
just been telling me about it.).
I could best reveal my great interest and
continue to conceal my bewilderment by means
of a judicious question:
"What do you call your poem?" I asked.

The triangular mark on his forehead
was manifest suddenly as he looked at me
eagerly, dramatic, incredulous.
He spoke; though in a low voice which was
hardly audible at times above the odd, snorting
sound made by Waves of the Sea in his even
satisfaction.

"I take my poem in my arms;
I hold it tight in the calms of night.
I take my poem's hand and run;
we laugh and play all the sunny day,
and yet my poem, soft, close and light,
is nameless as the faraway
— as nameless as the out-of-sight;
and I am shameless as the day is long
to be in love with a nameless song.

When the moon is new
and the woods are blue
and the waves on the sea are thin,
then my poem fades
in the breathing shades
and the Ghosts of Doubt walk in.

When the moon is full
we can feel its pull
and so can the ocean waves.
Then my poem and I
to the ghostyard fly
and go hopping across their graves.

So I'll name it after a moonbeam, soft and light,
because I understand it best at night;
or I'll name it after the oceans, wide and deep
because it never goes to sleep . . . . "

Loud, — low, ebb and flow;
low as the moan on dying lips
then clear and shrill as a knife in the sky,
his voice and mind,
already one, self-intertwined and gone away,
came back again to stab my peace,
(half-formed
like smoke yet in the pipe unpuffed).

Half dreaming in the silent shroud of lacy green
                    and blue reflected;
half dreaming of a monastery, hazy, seen through
fleckèd foam, occluding morning mist,
I'd hear his rising tale of moons and seas intruding:
then, as sure as firm, across his fitful rambling
came Nature's arm of quietude —
tranquillity of earth and leaf and stalk to overcome
                    his shouting
while I continued walking in my thoughts,
undisturbed as though he never was;
undisturbed because
I wished it so.

I thought of the little men and what they were.
I wondered how they wrote their clever songs.
I wanted more than anything to write one too.

I'd write of the sea and the wind and the rain
and the sunset sky,
or the whirring, purring, tuneless tune
of a chirruping grig;
I'd write of the tree and the window-pane
and the passers-by.
or the Big Man's echoing funeral.

Yet all of these are common things.
I ought to write as Double Faggot writes:
of sparrows growing griffons' wings
or the million lives in a comet's tail,
of ivy choking haughty city heights
or the track of a snail.

I wanted more than anything to write a song;
a moment's urge – no more – yet strong: as strong
as moment's anger, moment's fear or hate,
and here between too early and too late

(which have no inbetween)
I saw the face I'd seen before
when first we found the Door.

"Which is worse, homunculus:
to be too early and so full of madcap impulse,
empty of experience;
or be too late and, bursting with the necessary
                         wisdom for success,
to lack the vital spark, ambition?
There is no inbetween . . . "

So taunted the face.

Desperately I looked about for inspiration.

A drove of tireless lissom polliwigs came darting
into view
from the dimness of the pool.

I drew my line at once in desperation:

   "O tadpole,
        writhing, eating, living so;
       why must you grow
          to be a
            toad?"

Double Faggot's impassioned muttering had subsided
gradually and by now ceased altogether.
I regarded him, achievement bright in mine eyes.
He blushed . . . . I knew not why,
nor cared.

"Oh why is everything so kind
and why am I so happy now?
Oh why is it I never find
this perfect mood just when and how
I ask for it?

Why, oh why is everything so beautiful?"
No answers to my thought,
except the rumours of the waterfall
and the cry of the worm that the wren had brought
to feed her young.

Proud, clear and silent as a stone
that day stood forward and let all others by,
that limpid, memorable day I spent alone
as sorrowful yet joyous as the sigh
of parting lovers.

Stirring softly there beneath a reapers' moon
were rippling melodious Fortune and Fancy's fragile
                        harmonies
combined, their hearts' engrossed cocoon
of mystery spun mutely, unobtrusively by soothing
                        rhythmic tendril
sweeping, swaying, restless — deep
against the sky.
Music was rife as I fell asleep
in love with life, in love with love.

Inexorable Time above
looked down, and saw me from his leaping star.
He'd never wished before,
but now he wished and from afar
I saw the great wide-circling arc of light
as Time himself came sailing through the night
to join me there.

He glanced around the spangled glade
and smiled on Double Faggot nodding in the shadow.
Then curling up contented — lotus-eyed,
he fell asleep, unbreathing, close beside me.

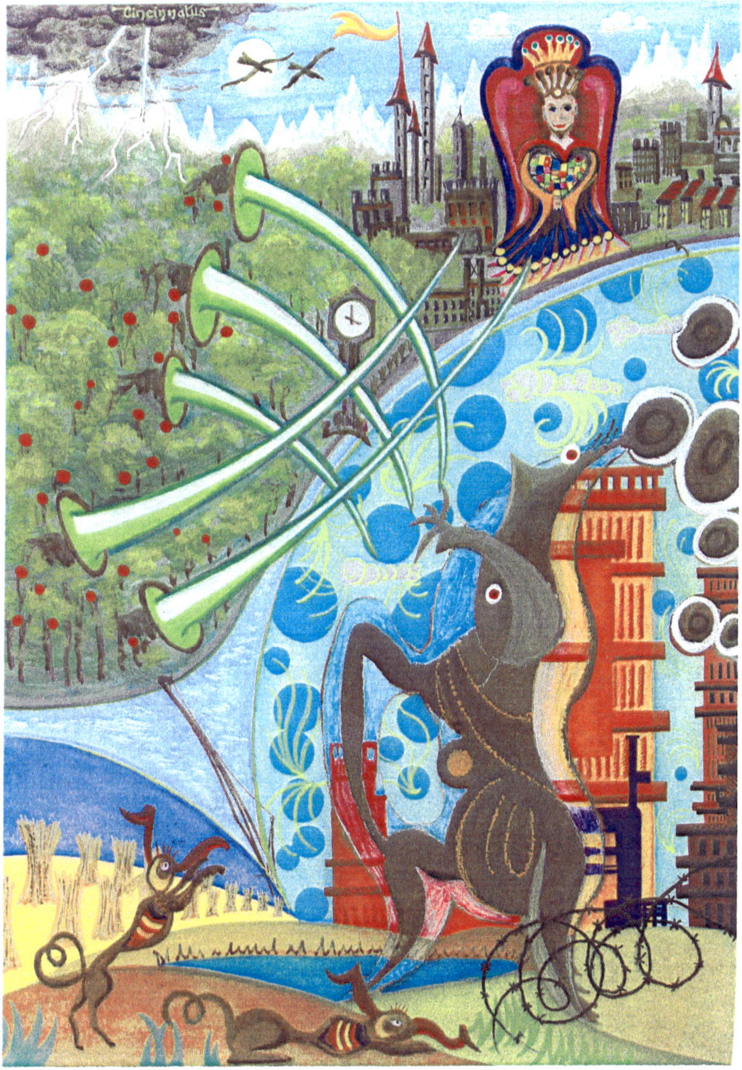
Cincinnatus

II

      I was awakened by someone shaking me;
shaking me so roughly that my teeth
chattered like do cartwheels over cobblestones.
Unbroken — not cracked either, nor even irreparably
bent — I looked up at mine assailant. It was
Trog; Sam Trog. He said so distinctly through
the mist in mine ears:
"I'm Trog," he said distinctly,
"Sam Trog.
and hurry please.
You're to meet the Prince."

The pool was there and the stream, just as
when I had fallen asleep.
But I had been alone
and the trees were gone, though I had hardly
time to observe this much even before I
was whirling across the undulating plain
behind the mysterious Trog.

We followed the course of the stream;
it became a river and still we went on
until a great city came in sight ahead
with many bridges.
Waiting by himself on the nearest bridge
stood a gaily dressed young man wearing a coronet.
"This is Prince Cosmo Parhelion III of Cosmopolis,"
announced Sam.
"How d'ye do," I said.
"I'm *very* well, thankyou," answered the Prince.

We stayed there for some time admiring the
view of the city (or was it two cities
with the river flowing between?).

"That is Cosmopolis," said Prince Cosmo, waving
his arm proudly over the left bank.
"And that is Troglodion," said Sam, indicating
the other.

Cosmopolis . . Troglodion;

Troglodion, Cosmopolis . . .
the same — a mile apart
the most and closely linked by bridges;
three or more,
five or more,
 . or more.
from one of which the Great Hall
and the Great Hall Clock
dominate the world
(shifting slightly
in the shimmering heat).

The Great Hall Clock chimed sweet sixteen
as I lay me down on the green
grass bed by the pool.
A pathetic fool
passed by in the dream I dreamed
(in the middlemost dream)
where everything seemed
wide awake — all agog;
not as clumsy
as a clog

nor as careless
as the scrawling finger;
but more naïve,
more remote,
like a many-coloured goat
or a fan
or a caltrop.

[Why! they even stick newspaper on!]

The pathetic fool began
to chop the sticks of day
and I ran away.

The Great Hall Clock struck twenty three
as I climbed the tree,
the precarious tree by the pool.
The pathetic fool
had gone his way
from the dream I dreamed
(from the middlemost dream)
and everything seemed
clear cut — a little harsh;
not as hazy

as the marsh
nor as lazy
as the sleeping helmet;
but more obscure,
dimly seen,
like unfathomed reason,
inordinate desire
or the purple fire
in the deep glass jug of hippocrene.

The pathetic fool was lean and shy
as he passed me by
and he'd whispered "why?
oh why? . . oh why?,"
so there by the stream
with Time at my side
in the middlemost dream
and the inbetween
I could only hide.

The Great Hall Clock boomed a hundred-and-one
and I knew that the time of trial was done . .
(though it was'n't until the umpteenth stroke
that I awoke).

As I thought after this wise, we had moved
from the first bridge and were walking down
the embankment towards the bridge on which the
Great Hall stood. As we walked they told me
of their cities; of Cosmopolis, as old as the
hills themselves, and of Troglodion, younger
than many a man.

Sam Trog began:

"Fifty two years ago,
when mediocrity flourished above all things
and a narrow mind
was fashionable,
a man of imagination
came to light in Cosmopolis;
a man outside convention,
an unorthodox man
whose occupation and delight
was the systematic ridicule
of the more fatuous principles
and ideals of his time.

He was cast down, suppressed,
only to rebound
and attack with fearful vigour
and effect
even the most inviolable, incontrovertible
axioms of the day.

Tall, ephemeral weeds
sprang up where his feet touched
and dogs, erotic mongrels,
capered in his wake.

He was banished
to the other side of the river
and his followers followed.

A colony was founded:
the first Troglodion.

The man was wed to his inspiration
and children were conceived —
brought into being profusely,
in greater or less degree
deformed,
yet always endowed with
something of the imagination
or vitality
of their sire.

And the dogs multiplied
proportionately
and the erotic weeds.

The city state of Troglodion
has grown in fifty years

to the same stature
and maturity
as had its fractious parent.

I am proud to be today's Representative.
Yesterday it was someone else;
tomorrow yet another
if tomorrow comes."

It was Prince Cosmo's turn:

"My ancestor,
a noble man
(with shaggy eyebrows
and a simple taste),
came down an age ago
from the hills
to this place
which was then a waste land.
He built a fortress,
a hospital, a library,
a college
and a cathedral
besides the homes for his people.

That was the first Cosmopolis.
The place was peaceful
and it prospered
through the middle years.

Then occasional wars
and pestilence
reduced the standards,
and the small evils
gained a hold.
Poor things flourished
and a civil hate sprang up.
Life was at a lower level.

My great great grandfather, Cosmo,
well-intentioned though he was at first,
made a mistake.
He built encircling high frustrating walls
instead of balanced bridges,
and in his strutting pride before the fall
ignored the swelling ridges
which precede the mount.

He tripped and fell and picked him up,
and at the golden Lethean fountain
filled to the brim the blinding cup
of cool conceit
and drained it.

My grandfather
changed all that,
but too late —
the line had acquired
a bad reputation
which persisted until
my father's recent reign.

During the bleak period
of a half century ago
the city split
and it was the better part
which broke away.

The recoil after this break
set our city
back in its exact place
and we prospered again.

The evil minority was a
minority once more.

Yet always our people have doubted
the Troglodytes
for the dogs and weeds.

And the Troglodytes scorn
us for the few
among us who persist in
the old, rotten beliefs.
Our tradition only
is our strength
in their eyes.

In our eyes
their freedom only
is their strength."

We were at the bridge now, and climbing
the steps to the balcony of the Great Hall,
which overlooked the road and the river
rolling under.

"Now for the show," said the Prince, and he
raised his arm: this was the signal for two
trumpets to sound out: which in its turn
was the signal for two processions to march
forward onto the bridge — from the left the
Troglodytes and from the right the Cosmopolites.

They continued at a steady pace, passing each
through the other in front of the Great Hall
in ordered confusion.
It was a fascinating sight:

I saw the freckled youth of the piercing eye
      and the unkempt hair;
I saw the crouching figure of Grief
      in a high-backed chair;
I saw the children of Who? and Why?
      When? How? and Where?,
and I saw the Beyondbelief.

I saw the chuckling old weatherman there and the Race
      and the Child-who-is-Lame;

I saw the trundling, whimpering Boy with a Cart
        in conspicuous shame;
I saw that Sam Trog had tears of pride on his face
        as his carnival came
        by the Great Hall steps,
and I saw what was in his heart.

I saw the empty double tressure flory-counterflory vert
        in the chief point sinister;
I saw the democratic demi-lion sneak away in
the white, starched, diamond-studded, diplomatic shirt
        of a cabinet minister;
I saw Prince Cosmo's cousin's friend's brother's butler's
wife as she went along pretending to be Marie Aintoinette
        — but in a greasy apron (for she had'n't
        changed, nor washed - had'n't finished her
        menial duties, even though she *s'était levée*
        before three just so that she may be
        ready in time)
and I saw that because of her
Prince Cosmo for the moment
was quite upset.

Reaching the opposite ends of the bridge, the
processions turned about and converged once more
on the Great Hall. Prince Cosmo and Trog had
slipped away as I watched this and now I
went down from the balcony to look for
them in the crowd which had gathered below.

But they were nowhere to be seen
and this time the processions marched slowly
side by side through the lofty doorway of
the Great Hall, separating inside to stand
forming a narrow aisle down the centre;
Troglodytes on the left, Cosmopolites to the
right. Behind them on each side, the excited
multitudes filled the Hall.
Everyone was packed in, leaving empty the
streets and buildings of two cities.

As the last of the crowd pressed his way in,
there was a sudden silence;
broken almost at once as two fanfares
simultaneously blared forth their different
and individual proclamations.

The Great Hall Clock struck One.

Prince Cosmo Parhelion III of Cosmopolis
and
Sam Trog of Troglodion
now appeared from a side entrance to march
majestically down between the ranks of
their peoples to the far end of the Great Hall
at the foot of the throne, where they
stood aside, each at the head of his
own column.

Silence again . .

I was wondering what would happen next
when someone pushed me forward and
whispered something unintelligible at mine ear.
I found myself walking down the narrow
avenue, the men closing in behind so that
I could not turn back.
I went right on past the Prince and Sam to
the foot of the steps leading up to the throne.
I mounted slowly, then turned to face
the assembly.

Sam Trog and Prince Cosmo marched up the steps.

They offered me each a casket. I accepted
them and they withdrew.

I opened Sam's first. Inside was a shimmering
rainbow-coloured mood. I shook it out to
its full extent and a million emeralds and
rubies flashed and glittered in the
dim lit Hall. There was a gasp of awe
and admiration from the Cosmopolites and a
violent burst of applause from the whole
assembly (excluding, of course, Sam Trog whose
work it was).

As the cheers subsided I opened the other box
— Prince Cosmo's; a dazzling array of
love-scented myths and chivalrous carved
fables tumbled out filling the Hall with their
fragrance.
Again tumultuous applause — then an expectant,
deathly hush.

I understood now.

I had to choose between them. I had to say
which was the better; and such a decision
was plainly impossible, for each was indescribably
perfect in its own way.

I was wondering rather nervously how I could
explain this to them, for they clearly were
beginning to show signs of impatience, when
there was an uproar without. The Hall
itself shuddered as though angry to be
interrupted at such a moment, and the air
was rent by heaving, thunderous noises.

Everyone rushed outside.

A fearful sight met us there.
The forests had marched from the mountains and
the earth shook as they smashed their way
through the city streets of Cosmopolis and
Troglodion both.

Panic stricken, the people who an hour before
had cheered onward a gay carnival procession

ran hither and thither to dodge and escape
annihilation.
Thousands were killed as the trees
tore down the traditions of Cosmopolis,
the freedom of Troglodion.

Then, when there was nothing
left big enough to destroy,
they turned on each other
and were themselves destroyed.

Dark, muttering birds
flew across the sun
and the choking atmosphere
flickered grimly
like little flames licking
a blackened window frame
and the sun went out,
extinguished by the storming clouds
which rolled after.
The World was lit only by
the lightning prongs plucking
at the higher places

and the weird shimmer
of spirits departing
in great hordes
to more clement hells.

Cold as death,
evil as death,
cold and evil a mighty breath
of raving mountain sky
swept down to the screaming valley
of havoc below . .

Slow . . slow . .
too feeble and slow
the living, creeping beings crept
to shelter, only to die
except for one predestined group
which found a cave —
Sam Trog, two men,
the Prince, two more,
dragged weary to the mountain shore
of that sea of mud and gore.

A month of storm
which was an eternity . . .

A month of calm
which seemed an eternity,

both adding only a moment
or less to our seven lives
and then . .

And then the first new dawn
and the first new day
of awakening;
of resurrection;
of reconstruction
after a complete devastation.

Spaces were cleared
bounded not by fence nor wall
but only by the uncleared spaces,
which that day diminished
as the sun increased.

Pastures and life, commerce, cities
and art sprang up as the sun
increased and diminished
on the first day
after the storm.

The Prince, assured, confident,
ran swiftly out along
his previous established rails
supported on every side by
sure precedent.

Trog pulled with prodigious energy
in three opposite directions,
pounding, pounding on the stubborn earth
and moving spasmodically, erratically,
unpredictably nowhere.
He stopped,
debating the method
of best coordinating the three
great forces at his disposal.

They spun wildly
together in a ring of indecision

churning the protesting earth
to a bog.

Sam Trog from the bog
cried "Help!" and I helped him;
I knew if I helped him
that others would too,
and they did, and they do.

[In twenty years' time he'll be out of the bog,
acknowledged by all, even men in the fog
of inartistic pedantry.]

As I left him there
and prepared myself for the journey back home,
his hand met mine
and he gave me a ragged ear of paper.
I paused in the fast-fading twilight to read it.
I read it;
but just as I finished a wind rushed by
which snatched the words from me
and took them on high
where I saw them change to a bird —
a firebird.

I could not remember the message I'd read;
I tried to remember — I tried and I try
and I reached for the firebird for only he knew
what the message had said
but still higher he flew,
and higher and higher right up to the sky.

Then back on the swirling breeze came a melody,
strangely and wistfully rising and falling:
it sounded to me
like a chorus of nuns
whose celestial music
was calling from far over sea.

Back and again comes the struggling memory,
plaintive and wistful it ever will haunt me:
the firebird's glim rhyme to help him along
on the dim wings of Time —
        a troglodyte song . .

Is it right or wrong?

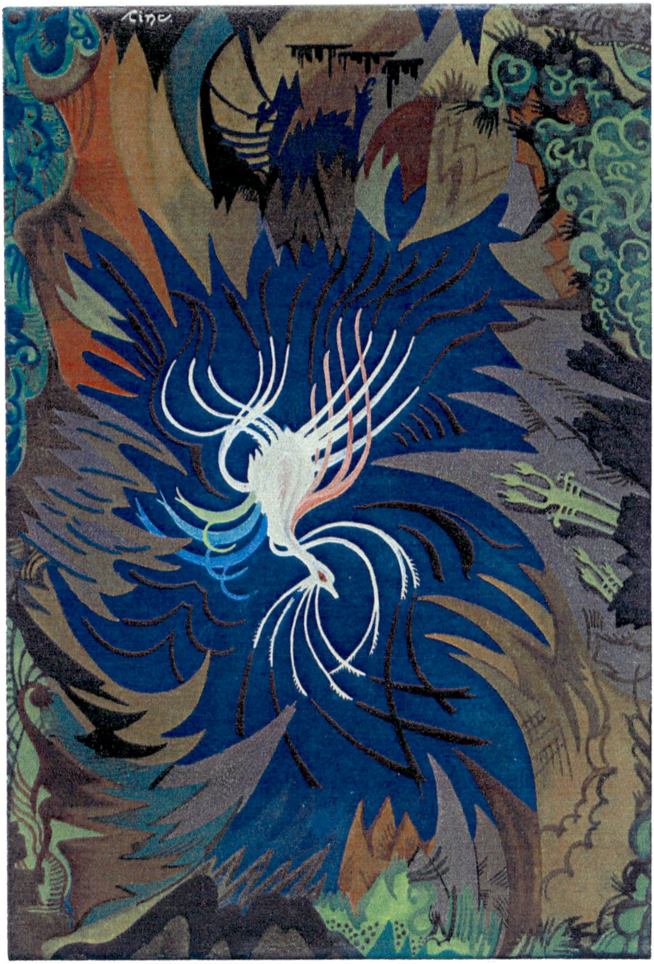